Dr. Sharon H. Porter

www.drsharonwrites.com

Next In line to Lead : The Voice of the Assistant Principal

Class of 2017! What's Next?

Women Who Lead: Extraordinary Women With Extraordinary Achievements Volume 1

Women Who Lead : Extraordinary Achievements With Extraordinary Achievements Volume 2 Featuring Latina Leaders

Women Who Lead in Education Volume 3 Featuring School Principals 1st Edition

Young Ladies Who L.E.A. D.

The Power of Networking: How to Achieve Success With Business Networking

North Carolina Girls Living In A Maryland World

Fifty & Fabulous The 2019 Edition

The HBCU Experience Anthology Volume 1 The North Carolina A&T State University Edition

The HBCU Experience Anthology Volume 2 Alumni Stories From the Hill of Kentucky State University

Women Who Lead In Education

Featuring School Principals

2nd Edition

Presented by

Dr. Sharon H. Porter

Copyright © 2021 Perfect Time SHP LLC

All rights reserved. No portion of this book may be reproduced, stored in a retrieval system, or transmitted in any form or by any means—electronic, mechanical, photocopy recording, scanning, or other—except for brief quotations without the prior written permission of the publisher..

For information regarding special discounts for bulk purchases or purchases by organizations, associations, and nonprofits, please contact the publisher: **Perfect Time SHP Publishing.**

info@perfecttimeshp.com

www.perfecttimeshppublishing.com

Published by Write the Book Now, an imprint of Perfect Time SHP LLC.

ISBN-978-1-7361028-3-1

DEDICATION

Women Who Lead Volume 3 Featuring School Principals 2nd Edition is dedicated to school principals across the globe. Whether you are a first year principal or have over 20 years of experience as a principal your journey to the principalship matters. We lead as we continue to learn.

Dr. Kendra D. March

As 'Women Who Lead' you are the epitome of excellence, compassion, and leadership! ~ Dr. Kendra March

FOREWORD

I am a public educator formally for 29 years and informally since the fourth grade. I have aspired to be a teacher since my formative years. I was blessed to have strong elementary school teachers I idolized, who made a lasting impression, and supportive parents who encouraged me to follow my passion. Growing up in Winston-Salem, North Carolina, I attended elementary, junior high, and high school with Dr. Sharon H. Porter. We were friends then and have since become colleagues and thought partners.

Congratulations to each of the 'Women Who Lead' represented in this anthology; hearing your calling and accepting your assignment as an Instructional Leader is worthy of celebration and recognition each and every day. Public education is by far the most challenging profession in our country with the most critical and long-lasting impact. During my tenure as a public educator, I have had the honor and privilege to be guided by special mentors who have helped me navigate my journey.

While professional learning and development provides training from textbooks, academic articles, research and other resources, I invite you to consider the role of public educators as the providers of equitable experiences, exposure, and opportunities for all students. Instructional leaders make hundreds of decisions on a daily basis, and it is crucial to remember that all decisions have consequences. At times, the decisions we make do not result in our intended nor expected outcomes. When this occurs, and it will, it is perfectly appropriate to make a different decision - particularly if you have gained additional information. My father, a retired educator, taught me that if you are going down the wrong path, you need to veer off and select another path. I keep that advice in mind in both my personal and professional life.

Entrance into any organization (school), for adults or children is correlated to satisfaction and successful outcomes. Staff recruitment, orientation, and evaluation, along with student onboarding at the school level, must be purposeful, intentional, and relevant. Hiring practices, such as candidate screening, resume' reviews, relevant questioning, and task completion; as well as real time observations are effective approaches in vetting prospective staff. Similarly, getting to know you activities, intentional family interviews, and goal setting are effective opportunities when welcoming new students to school.

As 'Women Who Lead' you are the epitome of excellence, compassion, and leadership! This can be exhausting. I encourage all who lead to practice intentional self-care. While not often discussed, it is vital in order for you to be your best for the school communities you lead. I implore us all to do things that make us feel good and that feel good to us. Do those things and do them often.

Women Who Lead in Education serves as a tool to utilize and grow our network. These female authors share the intimate realities of their experiences as public educators. I again applaud Dr. Sharon H. Porter and the collective of brilliant authors represented here for your outstanding work. You are changing lives. I am especially proud of Dr. Sharon for her continued vision of "Lifting As You Climb" - my personal and professional mantra!

Dr. Kendra D. March

About Dr. Kendra March

Dr. Kendra March, a native of Winston-Salem NC has served In Guilford County Schools as the school support officer for Elementary Area 2 since 2017.

March started her educational career in Charlotte-Mecklenburg Schools (CMS), as a classroom teacher and then served as an assistant principal and principal. In CMS, she led Elizabeth Traditional, Crestdale Middle, Hopewell High followed by being asked to return as the principal of Westerly Hills Academy, a high-poverty, struggling school as part of "Strategic Staffing Initiative" which her dissertation was based upon.

Under March's leadership, student proficiency grew more than 23 percentage points on state tests, and the school's growth designation changed from "no recognition" to "high growth" status. The North Carolina Department of Public Instruction named Westerly Hills a "School of Excellence" due to the high-growth standards.

Dr. March has also served in central office and state level positions in Georgia, New York and North Carolina as a school transformation coach, assistant superintendent, and deputy superintendent.

March has her bachelor's, Master's Degrees in School Leadership and K-12 Curriculum and Instruction and Supervision, and her Doctorate in Educational Leadership, all from the University of North Carolina-Charlotte.

Table of Contents

ACKNOWLEDGMENTS 1

CHAPTER 1 Staying In The Room 3

CHAPTER 2: The Power of Collaboration in Instructional Leadership: My Journey 13

CHAPTER 3: Our Diversity, Equity and Inclusion Journey 25

CHAPTER 4: Lifting As We Climb: My Journey in Educational Leadership 38

CHAPTER 5: Purposed to Lead During Difficult Times 47

CHAPTER 6: Leading From My Core 57

CHAPTER 7: The Principalship 67

CHAPTER 8: Built To Last: Creating A Culture And Climate Of Excellence 75

CHAPTER 9: The Secret Ingredient to A Successful School - A Great Culture 89

VISIONARY AUTHOR 101

ACKNOWLEDGMENTS

I would like to acknowledge the amazing educators who have made this 2nd Edition possible:

Foreword Author: Dr. Kendra March

Contributing Authors:

Ms. Trelane Clark
Dr. Sheka Houston
Dr. Alicia Maphies
Dr. Alana D. Murray
Mrs. Kristina Pollard
Ms. Shawaan Robinson
Mrs. Jewel Sanders
Mrs. Tammy Taylor
Dr. L. Jackie Tobias

Ms. Trelane Clark

My experiences as a Black woman in education have fueled my passion to learn about and strive for equity and representation in schools.
~Trelane Clark

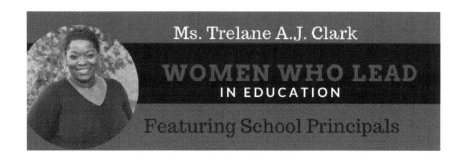

CHAPTER 1

Staying In The Room

By Ms. Trelane Clark, M.A.T., C.A.G.S.

You're going to walk into many rooms in your life & career where you may be the only one who looks like you or who has had the experiences you've had. But you remember that when you are in those rooms, you are not alone. We are all in that room with you. - Vice President-Elect Kamala Harris

As I sat with my six-year old daughter watching the then Vice President-Elect, Kamala Harris deliver this quote in her acceptance speech, I suddenly felt surrounded by all the Black women to whom I believed Kamala was referring. Mary Jane Patterson. Mary McLeod Bethune. Daisy Bates. Charlayne Hunter Gault. Katherine Johnson. Marva Collins. I thought about all of the rooms that I have and continue to walk into every day, scanning the room for someone who even remotely looks like me, and hoping they see me seeing them in our black womanness; there to occupy space; there to sit at the table.

As I write this chapter, we are experiencing the COVID-19 pandemic. The devastation of this pandemic is not easily put into words. It has forced us to give up many of the freedoms we enjoyed. We lost loved ones, jobs, security. However, there are two sides to every coin. The pandemic forced us to stop, slow down, pay attention, listen, look, and learn, mostly about things that many were choosing not to deal with -- racial and social injustice, educational and health care inequities, the fragility of our economy and its ability to rob us of our livelihood. Quarantining allowed me to become laser focused on my passions, my personal and professional goals, my family and learning to enjoy life. One of those passions I have been zeroing in on is working to ensure that I see not only myself but also other Black women in education thrive.

Before I knew what it meant to have a seat at the table, before I knew that there were efforts to keep me from the table or even entering the room, I was already there. It's almost as if I have been groomed for this my entire life. In fifth grade, I was the only Black girl in my class and even in a few classes below me. In high school, I was the only black girl in my freshman class and one of two and a half in my graduating class. The world opened up a bit more at the predominantly white all women's college where I was amongst an array of Black women of the diaspora sprinkled throughout the campus. I told myself that when I became a teacher I would see more teachers and principals who looked like me. However, I found myself in my first teaching position as one of two black teachers in a school with predominantly Latinx students and staff.

There is a wide body of research out there about the impact of being the only one of your race or ethnicity in schools and workplaces. Of what I have learned, I can certainly attest to much of its validity. It is hard to be the only black woman in a room no matter what other race of people sits in the room with you. Yet, it is not impossible to occupy that seat and to use the space that you occupy to influence and effect real, enduring change. We know this from the heroines who've gone before us and those still among us who do it every day. Because this has increasingly become the norm for Black women in the United States, we must shift the conversation towards making space for and supporting one another while we are in the rooms.

My experiences as a Black woman in education have fueled my passion to learn about and strive for equity and representation in schools. Diversity, equity and inclusion (DEI) have become ideals that schools and many other workplaces are making space for in their mission and vision statements, improvement plans and hiring policies and practices to the extent of hiring employees whose job title demands a strict focus on this area. These are great steps to take only if our schools are held accountable for putting effort behind changing policies and practices. I believe it is our responsibility, those of us who are in positions of influence, to seek that accountability. As a teacher and an assistant principal, I often volunteered to serve on hiring committees with the hope and the goal of ensuring that a voice of the underrepresented was heard in the room. As a principal, I now have the level of influence that I need to seek and hire from a more diverse candidate pool that reflects the racial, ethnic, and cultural backgrounds of the students I serve. That process includes having conversations about the importance of diversifying our staff with my leadership team, revising our interview questions to address not only pedagogical knowledge, but also mindset about our student demographics and culturally responsive teaching. It involves asking current staff to refer candidates for open positions, reaching out to community organizations, and even my own personal connections to generate interest and ultimately new hires. Additionally, in order for those individuals to stay in the room, we have to focus on retention, providing the support, so that they feel so connected to the community that they want to stay and grow with it. I believe that part of my role as a Black female school leader is to open doors and provide opportunities for others who do and do not look like me in order to create a more just, equitable school community.

For many years, I tried to downplay my existence as a Black woman amongst faculty of predominantly white educators, but it was impossible. My chocolate brown skin and my various hair styles are a dead giveaway. I tried to downplay my educational achievements, but I couldn't. My intellectual acuity and the degrees on my wall are a dead giveaway. I tried to downplay my ability to influence others, but it's not easy. The way I can change the atmosphere of a room when I walk in is a dead giveaway, I've been told. Each of these facets of me has played a role in how I have had to maneuver through white workspaces in schools. This is not me being haughty--these are examples of how microaggressions and micro assaults have shown up in my life that I have either contested or regretfully, ignored as a Black woman school leader.

In many leadership roles, I have felt the need to negotiate with myself just how much of my Black self I could bring to my work. Looking back on my earlier years in leadership, I can see how I tried to conceal or minimize my Black womanness. I tried to render my Black womanness invisible by either not addressing it or steering clear of conversations that would highlight it. I just wanted to be seen for who I am. I would observe other Black women and women in my family who brilliantly navigated workspaces deeply entrenched in upholding their institutionalized racist tendencies, workspaces that checked another box by hiring them but had little to no interest in creating more equitable work environments. I often wondered to myself, how does she do it? If I had the opportunity, I would just ask her! While I can't recall specific words of wisdom bestowed upon me over the years, I can say that the belief, energy, positivity and pride that has been shared with me has undergirded and fueled my ability to stay in rooms. How I choose to present myself unfortunately has no bearing in terms of how others choose to see me or if they choose to see me at all - cue the colorblind colleague. I have received advice to the tune of not wearing certain hairstyles, certain types of clothing, colors, not using certain words or phrases. On the contrary, many successful women have encouraged me to bring all of who I am into the room with the knowledge that although some aspects of me may not be expected nor accepted, I have the right to bring my knowledge and expertise into that space. Evolving into a consciousness where my work and my passion for it enters the room before I do continues to be a journey that I enjoy daily.

My Inspiration

As a woman who leads, my godmother, a veteran teacher, was the muse that led me into education. She invested time in me, saw my leadership potential at a very earlier age and fostered that growth by providing me with opportunities to lead. Additionally from every principal I have worked with as a teacher and as leader, I have extracted nuggets of wisdom as well as examples of mistakes that I have blended into my own unique leadership personality,

To Lead You Must Continue to Learn

Continued growth is imperative in leadership. Over the last two years, I have invested time and energy into building a professional learning network that is as broad as it is wide and is ever expanding. Connecting with other school leaders across the country and even the world has been some of the best professional learning I have ever done. To accompany those connections, I am a frequent conference, summit, workshop, and webinar attendee, an avid reader and listener of podcasts. While these activities support my overall growth as a person and as a leader, the day-to-day interactions with my students and staff are what truly support my growth and development as a leader, as their needs become my needs, and their successes become my joy.

There is no magic potion to drink, pill to take or pixie dust to sprinkle that will make it easier for Black women to stay in the room. There are some concrete strategies that have supported me on those days when my feet were pointed towards the door. These tips are not necessarily revolutionary, but, used with intentionality, can help us access the strength within us to "handle" it Olivia Pope style:

1. Vocalize your why - Go beyond just remembering why you do the work you do. Remind yourself daily. Tell your colleagues. Say it in meetings with and without using the word 'I.' Write it down. Share it with folks outside of education. Vocalizing our why breathes fresh air, which is essentially breathing new life into it every time it is projected into the atmosphere.

2. Keep the 3Hs in alignment- The 3H's are the Head, Heart, and Hands. Keep your head filled with knowledge of self and others, maintaining a learning stance of your own is the best way to model this for others. Keeping your head in alignment also speaks to your mental health. Practicing self-care strategies, stating affirmations, engaging in mindfulness activities are some ways of maintaining a healthy sense of self. Check your heart to make sure that you love those you serve and that you are operating in love and compassion for them. If your heart does not break for the things that break their hearts, it may be time to move on. Try to ensure that your hands are used as instruments to bring forth your mission and vision. It's not only what your hands physically touch, but it's also the places where you have influence.

3. Find your tribe - Intentionally seek out other Black women who are in the trenches with you. Share your story. Listen to theirs. Do life together with them. Affirm one another as you together lead your schools and organizations toward success.

It's almost like the lightbulb went on one day. I've learned that staying in the room has more to do with how I see myself than how others do. I realized that my own efforts to downplay my Black womanness were the obstacle to me not being seen for who I am. Today, this is no longer an option, as it does not serve me nor the people in the room with me. My goal is to not only have access to the room, not only to have a seat at the table in the room, but also to stay in the room.

About Trelane Clark

Ms. Trelane Clark is currently the principal at Hooks Elementary School in Chelsea, Massachusetts, a small city adjacent to Boston. She has been serving students and teachers in the field of education for almost 24 years, including nine as an assistant principal. Trelane embarked on her teaching career in the Boston Public Schools and has since served students in public, private, urban, and suburban schools in Virginia, Washington, DC, Boston, and its surrounding areas. She believes that building relationships and making connections with students and adults is central to the work that educators must do and credits the modeling of this to her own teachers and work experiences. Principal Clark's professional mission is to inspire educators to THRIVE- Teach from the Heart, model Resiliency, lead with Integrity, Value relationships, and ensure Equity for students, families, and educators.

Dr. Sheka Houston

"... I have learned that being a strong instructional leader is something that can greatly impact the achievement level of a school." ~ Dr. Sheka Houston

CHAPTER 2:

The Power of Collaboration in Instructional Leadership: My Journey

By Dr. Sheka Houston

I recently pressed submit on my final submission for my dissertation research study through Gardner-Webb University and that was the most exhilarating feeling. As a wife, mom, and middle school principal, conducting research on the comparison of impoverished schools in South Carolina that are performing well and impoverished schools in South Carolina that are not performing well was not an easy task. Some days, I felt so overwhelmed with it all. My two young daughters, Elizabeth and Isabella, served as my greatest inspirations. I wanted them to see me accomplish a great goal, so that they will know anything they set out to do is well within their reach. I could also hear the voice of my mom as a young girl telling me, "You've got to be somebody, so do well in school." I could see the eyes of my younger sister looking at me as she has looked up to me my entire life and I anticipated how I would feel celebrating such a great accomplishment with my biggest cheerleader and motivator, my husband. All of these things served as the fuel I needed to stay the course.

Through my research and my journey as a middle school teacher, assistant principal, and principal for the past eighteen years, I have learned that being a strong instructional leader is something that can greatly impact the achievement level of a school. There is mythical thinking surrounding this area in the education industry. That is the thinking that instructional leadership is not an area that can be developed in an individual, but that is absolutely not the case. My journey in education led to me becoming very strong in this area.

My school and practices are organized around four major themes: Leadership, Culture, Academics, and Systems. As the instructional leader of the school, I ensure that all stakeholders are included in the development of the mission, vision and focuses of the school. The mission of our school is to prepare student leaders to be college and career ready for success in a global society. The vision for our school is 1.5 years of growth or more for each student every year since many of our students come to us a grade level or more behind as they begin middle school. We focus on STEAM to ensure students are 21st Century Learners using a system called Learningblade.com. We cultivate leaders through our leadership initiative where students learn to take responsibility for their data and decisions and we succeed with the integration of AVID (Advancement Via Individual

Determination) strategies which are best practices teachers and students use to be most successful such as focused notes. Not only does the mission, vision and focus have buy-in from teachers, students and parents, they are all communicated effectively and regularly.

The culture of our school is driven and organized around Edmonds 7 Correlates of Effective Schools which my dissertation research is centered around. Dr. Ronald Edmond found schools that were high minority, high performing and high poverty to have seven things in common that he later called Correlates (Taylor, 2008). At the end of each year, I hold a staff meeting with the teachers and we organize our school and practices around the 7 Correlates:

1. Clear and focused school mission
2. Safe and orderly environment.
3. High expectations.
4. Opportunities to learn and time on task.
5. Instructional leadership.
6. Frequent monitoring of student progress
7. Positive home-school relations (Taylor, 2008).

My school has deliberate school-wide strategies in place for academic success that includes seventy-five minutes of bell to bell instruction for the four academic core areas of English language arts, math, science and social studies. English language arts and social studies teachers, as well as math and science teachers are paired to analyze NWEA data of students and together they devise and execute a plan that allows students' learning gaps to be addressed in all classrooms. This system serves as our multi-tiered system of support. We also utilize the workshop model and small group instruction in every classroom.

Finally, there are systems in place for teachers to collaborate by department, grade level and team. Our professional development on Tuesdays and Fridays are centered around our focuses and teachers have the opportunities to share best practices as the experts. In addition, model classrooms are designated within the school for other teachers to observe effective teachers in action and support systems are put in place for teachers that need it by the leadership team which includes two assistant principals and two instructional coaches in addition to myself.

I started my career in education as a career changer leaving the real estate and mortgage industries to become a business education teacher. When I started teaching business education, they hadn't developed standards for the course yet. My colleagues and I used the English Language Arts standards to plan our lessons and I collaborated frequently with a strong English teacher to plan engaging, meaningful lessons for students that reinforced the ELA content. I taught in that area for five years and was encouraged by an African-American, female assistant principal, who is now a friend, to pursue a role in administration, because she thought I was a natural leader. Not sure that I wanted to take that route, I attended a teacher leader initiative through the state department and it was something stated there that led me to take the leap. Being a natural problem solver, I noticed several of the problems in education, but never thought entering administration, at the time, was for me. However, in that state department session, the facilitator stated, "you can be a person that notices problems and talks about them, overlook them, or you can be a person that does something about them." I know that wasn't mind blowing, but it resonated with me at the right moment. From there, I added the administration certification to my master's degree to be eligible for an assistant principal position. I completed my internship ensuring I was filling in anywhere that I was needed and learning all that I could before school, after school and during my planning period. When the assistant principal position came open and I applied, I was honored to be selected to serve in that role.

I remained an assistant principal for eight years and during that time I had the pleasure of being mentored by a retired principal that was working with our school that saw something in me that I didn't see in myself at the time. The middle school I have worked in my entire career had several challenges. The environment was toxic, the students were not performing well, and we were a rural, Title I school. A school with this many challenges that is not performing, can really make you feel insecure and wonder if the decisions you are making will become impactful to student achievement and engagement. My mentor gave me the reassurance I needed and that gave me a great confidence lift. The power of a mentor can be so impactful. The lift I needed led to me applying for the principalship when the position opened. I got the job!

Getting the job was an accomplishment, now the work begins. To combat the culture challenges it was imperative that the practices at the school changed in order for the trajectory of the school to change. Culturally relevant literature and training for teachers was also essential to ensure teachers could connect and build relationships with students. Students also needed to see themselves in literature and the curriculum in a positive light to make connections and feel empowered. Finally, an effective plan to communicate regularly with parents (positive note campaign), teachers (weekly newsletter with staff shout-outs and announcements) and weekly town hall meetings with students to set the focus, tone and expectation for the week.

I was very happy to have the experience of the assistant principalship before becoming principal, but I can honestly say, the principalship is a completely different position than that of the assistant principalship, and you don't realize that until you take the position. It's important to surround yourself with people who are not judgmental, but invested in seeing you grow as a leader. This is important , because you won't know everything going into the position and it's important for new principals to know that…not knowing everything is ok.

My first year as principal was a smooth transition. I had worked at the same school as a teacher and assistant principal, so I knew the school, the parents, and the community. What I wasn't prepared for was my assistant principal being promoted to a principalship (which it was very deserving and I was very happy for him, but was a loss for me as a new principal) in the middle of the year, and having to replace 17 staff members (which was good for the culture shift that needed to take place) who were not buying into the new expectations and the vision that was in place to serve students and families to the best of our abilities. During this same time, the state adopted a change in the accountability model, so the first year, the school didn't receive a state report card, but the second year we did. We were ranked at the bottom, but not just the bottom, the bottom 10% which designated us as a Priority School. I was so disappointed. The only support I had, came from another principal, a friend from the district who was also ranked Unsatisfactory, but the bottom 5 percent which designated her school as a Comprehensive Support School where a state representative was assigned to provide support. We were both dumbfounded. How did we get here? I know what you are thinking…. "Birds of a feather flock together." This definitely wasn't us. We didn't stay down long and lick our wounds, we immediately sprang into action. We were not these rankings and neither were our teachers, our students, or our community, which was the same community we graduated from, so we knew better.

The first thing we had to do was a root cause analysis to get an exact measure of where we were and what got us there. One very important part of the root cause analysis is to examine the data of the school completely. The next step was to develop a strategic plan that would help us improve our status. Examining the data, we discovered that we were in line in most categories with the district, but not with the state. We knew we needed to do some things differently to obtain different results. In the root cause analysis, we also discovered that most of our students come to us from the elementary school one to two years behind. When students arrive at middle school and we teach them on grade level standards they are not yet ready to receive, this is why they would fall farther and farther behind. Not only were students not growing academically, their behavior was less than standard. Several things were needed to rectify these challenges. Students on the cusp were the students that would make the greatest impact on student achievement. We utilized a set curriculum to target their improvement that focused on strategies for writing, inquiry, collaboration, organization and reading. The other students needed interventions by their teachers using specific interventions aligned to the norms referenced test they take three times per year to help fill the gaps in their learning. I ensured teachers were trained how to do this and hired a math and literacy coach to provide more support to teachers. When I replaced the 17 staff members, several of the replacements were international teachers from Jamaica and the Philippines who were very strong in their content areas.

To improve behavior we used a program that focused on the social and emotional needs of children and hired a behavior interventionist to support teachers and students. We also utilized a strategy to determine if the initiatives put into place were impactful . Lastly, cultural relevance had to be addressed since 87 percent of our student population received free and reduced lunch and 70 percent of our population were African-American students. We needed to ensure that students saw themselves in the curriculum, around the school and in literature. We brought in a powerful speaker that gave students a true picture of their history, informing them that their history did not start with slavery and led the staff in a very powerful professional development session to use best practices and strategies while teaching.

In the end, with the support of one another, my school went up two report card grades and my "Trust Mate" advanced three report card grades. From fall to winter on the norms referenced assessment we increased from the 17th percentile to the 90th percentile in one grade level in reading. Finally, my middle school also won the STEAM School of Excellence Award by the Palmetto State Arts Education Association. Things definitely turned around for both schools.

Many people describe the principalship as lonely, and it can be, but my "Trust Mate" and I ensured it wasn't and our collaboration led to school improvement, and the creation of a powerful online platform called *The Collaborative* that brings educators, families, and authors together each week with story time. The platform promotes literacy from which we have also formed multiple community partnerships and a powerful book for new school leaders, leaders in school improvement and honestly any school leader who would like a guide on best practices for success entitled, *It Doesn't Have to be Lonely at the Top. The Power of Collaboration in Leadership* that can be purchased at www.CreateandEducate.Solutions beginning in March of 2021. We also provide professional development in literacy and strategic planning through our coaching practice Create and Educate, LLC. We have even had multiple requests to present at universities. I used to wonder why a former principal used to have such a perplexed look while serving in his position. A very stressful look. I don't wonder anymore, but I do have a solution for that look and it is called collaboration, a powerful strategy that can be the difference between success and failure.

Reference

Taylor, B. (2008). Effective schools process. Https://foresternet.lakeforest.edu/academic-resources/library/arvhives/history-of-effective-schools

About Dr. Sheka Houston

Dr. Sheka Houston is a passionate educator that has the desire to inspire all she comes into contact with to become the very best versions of themselves. She has spent the last 17 years in public education, 12 of which has been in administration. Sheka is currently the principal of a rural middle school in the southeast where she is entering into her fifth year of service to her community in this role. Her experience is unique in that Sheka works in the same district she graduated from and has been promoted from teacher to assistant principal and finally to principal all within the same school. Sheka also serves on the Board of Girls on the Run, Tri-County, South Carolina, serves as a Girl Scout Troop Leader, serves on the Juneteenth Celebration Committee and is a proud member of Delta Sigma Theta Recently, Dr. Houston conducted research to complete a doctoral program in educational leadership from Gardner-Webb University. Her topic; *Impoverished Schools that are Performing Successfully in South Carolina. How do They Differ from Impoverished Schools that are Underperforming?* was inspired by her desire to find solutions for new principals, especially those serving in high poverty areas, to experience success in the area of academic achievement for students.

Sheka has been married for 22 years and she and her husband have two beautiful daughters, Elizabeth and Isabella who are truly her inspirations, as she leads through the lens of a mom.

Dr. Alicia Maphies

"Don't let fear and intimidation stop you from pursuing a goal…"
- Dr. Alicia Maphies

CHAPTER 3:

Our Diversity, Equity and Inclusion Journey

By Dr. Alicia Maphies

I am the principal of a large 5A suburban high school in North Texas. We have approximately 2,100 students and 190 staff members. We are a rapidly growing school district, as we build a new high school of our size about every three years. Our campus demographics have greatly shifted in the twelve years that I've served here. In the past three years our campus has transitioned from being predominantly White, to being minority White. We are projected in the coming year to be approximately 42 percent Asian, 36 percent Caucasian 12 percent Hispanic and 8 percent African American. Our staff demographics, however, have not shifted quite as quickly. With this student demographic shift comes an obvious need for growth in cultural competence, an analysis of culturally relevant pedagogy, and an appreciation for diversity and inclusion.

Before I address our demographics further, I'd like to take you through the journey that brought me to this point in my career. My journey in administration and education has been a winding path. I began as a high school English teacher, French teacher and cheerleading coach in a low-socioeconomic campus in Southern California. I then moved to a mega high school in North Texas, and while teaching, I completed my Masters in Educational Leadership in anticipation that "someday" I would leave the classroom. That "someday" came much sooner than anticipated; the same year I finished my masters, I was offered a position as an Advanced Academics Coordinator, serving on a campus with both Advanced Placement and International Baccalaureate programs. After two years as an Advanced Academics Coordinator, I moved to a central office World Languages Coordinator position, and quickly realized that I still needed to be interacting daily with kids on a campus! I transitioned back to a campus as an assistant principal for eight years, and during that time I finished my doctorate in Educational Leadership and my Superintendent's certification. I was then afforded the opportunity to step into the campus principal position on the same campus where I served as an Assistant Principal for eight years. I have served as a campus principal for the past five years, including through our global pandemic.

Pivotal to my career, no matter the location, have been my mentors. My mentors have had a tremendous impact on me, particularly as a school leader. If you don't have a mentor – get one! Find someone in the position that you respect or desire, ask them if you can meet with them once a month for an hour, then ask questions and listen. When I was completing my administrative internship, I happened to know that my mentor had a lot going on in his personal life – his wife was battling cancer and son was in the hospital with health complications. Yet through this, I watched my mentor stand in the halls greeting his staff with a smile, stopping in classrooms asking how others are doing, and writing notes to lift-up the teachers for going above and beyond. These observations had a huge impact on my vision of what *servant leadership* means. *Servant leadership* is putting your own challenges and struggles aside to take care of those you support. You may have heard the phrase, "When the principal sneezes, the whole school catches a cold," it's a beautiful and true adage. Our role as leaders is to inspire our staff so that they can inspire kids. Be intentional that every conversation and every interaction lifts your people!

One of the most important decisions I've made as a school leader is to take calculated risks. Don't let fear and intimidation stop you from pursuing a goal – what's the worst that could happen? You struggle and learn from an experience? Great! For example, when I accepted my first role as Assistant Principal, I had no desire to leave my current school; I wanted to be an assistant principal in my current district, but it was clear that door was not going to open to me. I pursued a few opportunities outside of the district, and wound up in one of the top districts in the state. If I had let fear or near-sightedness impact me, I never would've left that original district. This lesson has carried me through so many other intimidating goals in my life, from pursuing a doctorate and defending my dissertation, to advocating for public education in the state capital with congressmen and senators. Each one of those experiences was initially intimidating and anxiety-inducing, and then turned into an incredible learning opportunity.

After earning my doctorate in educational leadership, I continue to learn and grow in my practice through multiple avenues, including our professional state principals' organization TASSP (Texas Association of Secondary School Principals), an incredible non-for-profit educational support group in Texas called Raise Your Hand Texas, the Deloitte Courageous Principals' Institute, through a women in leadership book study, and through my teachers on campus. I volunteer for every committee and opportunity through our state principals' organization that is available to me. Through this volunteerism, I've been provided stellar professional development on a multitude of topics over the years, and I've had an opportunity to interact personally with educational leaders such as George Couros, Ruby Payne, Jimmy Cases, Steve Gilliland and Dr. Michelle Borba. Get involved in your professional organizations, volunteer to serve on committees, say "Yes!" to every opportunity. My involvement in TASSP has then led me to the Raise Your Hand Texas Organization; this organization awarded me a grant to attend a summer professional development at Harvard, and invites me to a leadership institute every year where I continue to learn. I was also awarded a grant through our Regional State Service Center to attend the Deloitte

Courageous Principals' Institute, an enlightening weekend retreat that focuses on navigating diverse personality types, the goals of your institution, and effective communication. Lastly, I continue to learn daily from my teachers on campus. Anytime someone says, "Have you heard of..." my response is always, "Can you send me that article?" "Can we do a book study?" Or "Let's get together with your colleagues and talk about that!" My staff teases me that I say, "I love you" through "I saw this article that reminded me of our conversation..." Again, say "Yes!" to every opportunity – you never know what doors it will open for you.

I have multiple leadership gurus; some of my favorites are Brené Brown, Sheryl Sandberg and Simon Sinek. If you haven't read *Dare to Lead, Daring Greatly, Lean In, or Leaders Eat Last*, stop what you're doing, go order those books right now, and then come back to this. Go now! I've read each of these books, and so many more, through my women in leadership book study. We are a group of female educational leaders from all over the state who share a passion for learning and a willingness to be vulnerable and honest with one another as we grow. Our group is diverse in our roles, including teacher team leaders, a superintendent, an athletic director, and campus administrators; and that diversity is a huge strength in our contributions to one another. I highly recommend that you start a book study with 4-6 colleagues. The good news is, I've already given you a great book list to start!

Diversity, Equity and Inclusion

Now, to the meat of this chapter: with the rapidly changing demographics of our campus, coupled with the heightened political and social climate of our nation, diversity and inclusion are essential topics of discussion, focus and professional development for our team. As mentioned previously, our student demographics shifted quickly, and when the shift began, our campus staff was predominantly Caucasian; the staff demographic did not reflect the demographics of our students. If you haven't had the opportunity to research or read about the impact of students having teachers who look like them, it's an essential reading topic for all educators! Knowing this impact, it was a focus of our campus to bring quality candidates to our staff who represented our student demographics. We addressed staffing needs in our Campus Improvement Plan and talked about this need openly in collaborative forums. In the four years that I have been campus principal, our staff demographics have shifted from 5 percent Hispanic to over 12 percent Hispanic, matching our student demographics in this regard. We have more than doubled our percentage of Asian and American Indian staff on campus, and we anticipate that African American staff percentage now closely mirrors our student demographic as well. In addition, we were attentive to address the diversity and representation of our leadership staff and administrative team. That may not seem like a drastic shift, but it is a shift in the right direction, and with a very low campus turnover rate, it is progress.

The second focus with our shifting demographics was on staff professional development and cultural competence. With a majority Caucasian staff, I needed our staff to understand what it meant, for example, to be an African-American male in our society, the pressures that came with being a first-generation American high school student, or to be a Hindu student in a majority-Christian city. I formed partnerships with diverse community members and asked them to speak with our staff about raising a child in our community. For example, we had a LGBTQ advocate and lawyer speak with our staff about laws, pressures and suicide rates of LGBTQ students. We invited a representative from the local Hindu temple to share with us the potential cultural clashes of raising Asian-Indian children in suburban America. We welcomed a local Imam from a neighboring Muslim mosque to share the challenges of raising Muslim children in our society. Though there was serious reservation from some staff as to how this related to them as teachers, and these "talks" were not always received willingly, I ultimately had the majority of my teachers express that is the best professional development they've ever received.

Community partnerships also bridge the gap when our staff demographic do not reflect the demographics of our student population. We partnered with Alpha Kappa Alpha Sorority, Inc. for example, and invited them to meet on our campus. In exchange for a meeting space, the ladies volunteer to grade our Academic Decathlon team during mock interviews, register our students to vote during lunches, and judge our Speech and Debate students before they head off to state competition. In addition, we extended the partnership with our local Hindu temple, and they invited our teachers for a tour of the temple and to continue the discussion and dialogue about culture. We partner with local Homeowners Associations, to advertise our school events in a predominant language, and to encourage students to present or volunteer in our local communities; we've had HOSA, DECA and student-volunteer groups reach the community in this manner. When our students see us partnering with the diverse members of our community, it lets them know that we value their diversity and care about them as individuals.

To focus on our increasing diversity, we've also created a campus Diversity Task Force. This team is made up of administrative, counseling, teaching and district staff with a passion for equality in education. In the coming years it is our goal to add students to this committee. This diversity task force is focused on addressing the disproportionality of data that plagues most public schools in America, our campus included. Tragically, across our nation, students of color are often underrepresented in Advanced Placement courses and are overrepresented in instances of serious discipline such as In and Out of School Suspension or Discipline Alternative Education Placement programs. Our campus is no exception to this national data; however, I firmly believe that our campus is becoming a model for the solution! First, we trained our diversity task force and made them aware of the data on our campus. We attend Solution Tree trainings by Anthony Muhammad, which focus on how educator mindsets impact achievement gaps. Together we examined the political, economic and pedagogical practices that contribute to this achievement gap. This training led us to analyze campus policies and strategies that contribute to a superiority or victim mindset, instead of a needed liberation mindset. In addition, our counseling staff partnered with us to address the American School Counseling Associations Standards for Elimination Racism and Bias in schools, found at

https://www.schoolcounselor.org/asca/media/asca/Standards/RacismBias.pdf. Our task force was on fire and committed!

One of the first goals of the task force was to increase the representation of our minority students in Advanced Placement courses. We addressed this goal in our Campus Action Plan and provided opportunities for our staff to discuss how they personally own and impact this goal. We designated a teacher to 1) identify the students using AP Potential data from the PSAT test who could be successful in advanced courses 2) facilitate conversations with these students and their parents about their potential 3) partner and communicate with counselors to enroll them in at least one Advanced Placement course and 4) provide on-going support as they navigated the advanced course load. In addition, if any student wanted to drop an Advanced Placement course after signing up, we had them meet with their teacher and counselor to discuss the why, their fears and concerns, and how we could support them in remaining in the course. We made connections to Jim Collins' research, amongst others, indicating the level of rigor of courses in high school directly correlates to success in college. In our first year of this initiative, we increased the enrollment in advanced courses by Hispanic and African American students by 9 percent each!

Next, we sought to create a fire amongst a larger entity of our staff. Members of the diversity task force created a book study to further examine the pedagogical practices that contribute to the achievement gap, and they invited in staff members from across the campus. They began their book study with *White Fragility: Why It's So hard for White People to Talk About Racism*, by Robin Diangelo. I offered to purchase books for anyone wanting to participate in this book study, and we had nearly 30 staff members involved in our first book club, with a request to start another in the fall. Those originally 30 staff members completed the book study in the summer, also allowing them to earn non-contract professional development hours, a requirement of our district. In addition, this teacher book study prompted our National Honor Society students to initiate their own study, with student-led and teacher guided book studies occurring virtually across our campus.

We have also strived to create a culture on our campus that shows students the value and strength of our diversity. We've hosted fine arts diversity nights, where we share music from across the globe, art that highlights our diversity, and dance and dress that celebrate our cultures. Though small as this may seem, we have created a hashtag for our campus that is used on social media #StrongerTogether. This hashtag has taken off and has led to a twenty-foot by ten-foot mural on a wall of our campus, painted by our students, that boasts the value "Stronger Together". Our students hear the message after every lockdown, lockout or evacuation drill, that the best crisis prevention is before a crisis occurs; the most impactful action is creating a campus culture where everyone feels loved, valued, and that they have a place on our campus; we are so much #StrongerTogether. During my graduation speech in the wake of the George Floyd tragedy, I urged our students to share with the world what we already know on our campus, that they can transform "the way it's always been", the importance of compassion, that one small action can create incredible momentum, the power of their words and voice, the importance of their vote, and that we are so much "Stronger Together".

In addition, in the 2021-2022 school year, our district hired an Equity, Diversity and Inclusion Strategist to assist with these efforts across the district. Encouraged by this position, our campus will offer the first African American Studies course in our district's history. We are excited to pilot this course and be part of the curriculum writing and foundation of the course.

Though we have by no means "arrived" in our journey of campus culture as it relates to diversity and inclusion, we are certainly aware of our opportunities for growth, and we continue to work towards a campus of equality and opportunity for all students, no matter the color of their skin, income of their parents, or religion practiced in the home. The challenges are many, and we will continue to strive for this equity because we know our kids deserve it!

About Dr. Alicia Maphies

Alicia Maphies is the principal of a large 5A high school in North Texas. She holds a Bachelor's Degree from Michigan State University in English and Secondary Education, a Masters from California State University San Bernardino in Education and Curriculum, a Master's Degree from the University of North Texas in Leadership and Administration, and a Doctorate from Texas A&M-Commerce in Educational Leadership. Prior to administration, Dr. Maphies taught English and French, served as an Advanced Placement/International Baccalaureate Coordinator, and as a district Foreign Language Coordinator.

Dr. Maphies believes that her campus's mission to "develop critical thinkers who contribute positively to society" is at the core of all that we do, and this goal is only possible through communication and meaningful relationships. Dr. Maphies is married to Bobby, an officer in the United States Army, and together they travel the world to experience new sights, sounds, food, people and beliefs.

Dr. Alana D. Murray

"At the core of all strong principals is an understanding of instructional leadership and the intricacies of the life of a school." ~ Dr. Alana D. Murray

CHAPTER 4:

Lifting As We Climb:

My Journey in Educational Leadership

By Alana D. Murray, Ph.D.

The Beginning

I come from a family of educators. Both of my grandmothers were public school teachers in the Baltimore and Atlanta school systems. My mother served as an educational researcher at Johns Hopkins University and my father taught community organizing at the University of Maryland. I grew up amongst a group of amazing individuals who taught me to value public education.

However, initially I fought a career in education. I was a business administration major. I worked at Fortune 500 companies in the summer. I found this work unfulling. So, I began to be drawn to the work of education. While working in these companies, I also served as counselor for Maryland Leadership Workshops (MLW). MLW is a leadership development program focused on nurturing youth in public service. Serving as a staff member for this organization fueled my passion for teaching. At the end of my senior year, I decided to embark on teaching as a career. I received my Master of Arts in Teaching (MAT) from Brown University with a concentration in social studies. After my graduation, I was selected to serve as the Brown Summer High School co-principal for a summer. I worked with incoming student teachers and we created an amazing summer experience for Providence, RI high school students. The work was exhausting, challenging and life-changing. After that experience, I began to consider that maybe one day in my journey, school leadership might be an option.

Teaching Orientation

My first piece of advice for anyone interested in the principalship is to teach or have a position based in a school. At the core of all strong principals is an understanding of instructional leadership and the intricacies of the life of a school. For fourteen years, I taught social studies at both the high school and middle school levels. My favorite course was AP World History and I was part of the inaugural group of teachers who taught that course. In addition to AP World history, I taught National, State and Local Government (NSL), Latin American History, US History 8/9 and Seventh Grade World Studies. I served as a teacher leader in the capacity of a Seventh grade team leader and Social Studies department chair. It was in these teacher leader positions, I re-discovered my passion for leading and serving adults on behalf of children. I returned to my passion from college which focused on public administration. At this point in my career, I decided to pursue my administration certification.

Policy Orientation

My second piece of advice for aspiring school administrators is to develop an educational policy orientation. Throughout my teaching career, I stayed involved in educational activism beyond the classroom. Remember, you have summer off so volunteer in an organization that interests you!

During my first three summers as a teacher, I volunteered at Teaching for Change. Teaching for Change is a non-profit organization based in Washington DC which fights for eradicating oppression in education. This was unpaid labor but it was a labor of joy. My internship kept me steeped in shaping multicultural, anti-racist curricula and developing an understanding of organizing for community change. As a result of my work at Teaching for Change, at the age of 28, I served as co-editor for the book, *Putting the Movement Back Into Civil Rights Teaching*. I continued to be involved in policy discussions and the union in my school district asked me to create a certificate program steeped in issues of equity and excellence. Along with a colleague of mine, we co-created a five credit Equity and Excellence certificate program with McDaniel College, Montgomery County Education Association (MCEA), and Montgomery County Public Schools. We are celebrating our tenth year anniversary this year!

After completing the book, I pursued my doctoral education in minority and urban education at University of Maryland. My dissertation, which focused on African American women and the critical role they played in a co-creation of the alternative black curriculum in social studies, subsequently was turned into a book, *The Development of the Alternative Black Curriculum in Social Studies, 1890-1940: Countering the Master Narrative.* My scholarly work gave me a true appreciation of the issues that we need to address in order to close the achievement gap. I always say that the principal is the pathway to the larger work of a school system. It is vital that aspiring school leaders understand the intersection of practice and policy in order to improve student outcomes. Your system-wide impact is critical to your work as a principal.

The Work: Challenges and Joys

Although you work collaboratively as a principal, you have sole responsibility for the decisions related to building and maintaining your school. In my role as principal, I dealt with the death of a staff member, overhauled our school culture to focus on restorative justice practices, re-centered our equity work and built a vision for a diverse, multicultural community. I struggled with finding a balance between my personal and professional life. The COVID-19 pandemic provided my biggest adaptive challenge as we had to build a virtual school from scratch. However, I love the work. Being a principal, leading a community stimulates my mind as we work together to serve our students. The respect and gratitude you get from students, staff and parents inspires me daily.

Culturally Responsive School Leadership

For twenty-two years as an educator, the fight to close the opportunity gap for BIPOC students has been my north star. Being a principal allows me to shape the culture at my school to be strategically centered on equity. In Muhammad Khalifa's *Culturally Responsive School Leadership* he argued that school leaders need to demonstrate leadership behaviors built on critical reflection, generating culturally sustaining curricula and engagement with the community (12).

As a principal, I worked to have teachers reconsider oppressive school discipline practices. By incorporating restorative justice strategies, we reduced suspensions significantly in my school. I worked diligently to create community partnerships with our local church, The KID Museum (a children's museum and innovative maker space) and the National Symphony Orchestra. I've also continually engaged in the hard work of critical self-reflection. When I've struggled with difficult relationships with parents and students I've continually asked myself: What can I do to repair this relationship? I engaged in courageous conversations with staff members about decolonizing the curriculum. Principals must be brave and unrelenting in creating a new way to lead in public schools.

In conclusion, in the words of Mary Church Terrell, a famous black women activist, "And so, lifting as we climb, onward and upward we go, struggling and striving, and hoping that the buds and blossoms of our desires will burst into glorious fruition ere long." I hope by reflecting on my own leadership journey, you are inspired to begin your climb to school and district leadership.

Reference

Khalifa, M. (2018). *Culturally Responsive School Leadership*. Harvard Education Press.

About Dr. Alana D. Murray

Alana D. Murray, Ph.D. is an educator-activist who has taught world history on both the middle- and high-school levels and currently serves as a middle school principal at Shady Grove Middle School in Montgomery County, Maryland public schools. She has created pilot lessons on African American history, conducted youth leadership training workshops for several organizations and provided professional development to educators at conferences across the country. More recently, her research interests center on supporting principals in developing the skills to be culturally reflective school-based leaders. In 2005, she served as the co-editor of the publication, *Putting the Movement Back into Civil Rights Teaching* with Deborah Menkart and Dr. Jenice View. She is the author of *The Development of the Alternative Black Curriculum, 1890-1940: Countering the Master Narrative*. This book focuses on the impact of black women in shaping the social studies field.

Murray received a B.A. in government and politics from the University of Maryland, a M.A.T. from Brown University, and her PhD from the University of Maryland. Her work on this project stems from both professional and personal experience. She is the granddaughter of Donald Gaines Murray, whose landmark lawsuit against the University of Maryland Law School successfully desegregated the university. Her grandparents dedicated their careers to an equal education for all children and her parents instilled the critical roles of research and community organizing.

Mrs. Kristina Pollard

"Create an environment where people are recognized and celebrated for their success." ~ Kristina Pollard

CHAPTER 5:

Purposed to Lead During Difficult Times

By Mrs. Kristina Pollard

I began my teaching career two years after graduating from college. As a first generation college graduate I had the whole world sitting in front of me. I studied biology in hopes of becoming a doctor to fulfill dreams for myself and my family. After graduation, I quickly realized that going to medical school was not for me. I wanted to teach! I was able to enter an alternate route program and began teaching on the high school level. I loved teaching so much that I later went on to earn my master's degree in education knowing I needed to understand the methodology behind the art of teaching. I will never forget being home on maternity leave and taking a call from my principal encouraging me to apply for a teacher leadership position. It would allow me to provide professional development in the areas of instructional technology and make a huge impact on growthing our team. I humbly turned her down as I loved teaching in my classroom. Isn't it amazing that others can see in us what we do not see in ourselves? She was adamant that she needed my skills and that she saw purpose for me on her leadership team. Needless to say I came out of the classroom on what seemed like a jet into school leadership.

No one consciously steps into school leadership knowing they want to "fix" or transform schools. When I first began thinking of leaving my coveted classroom and stepping into leadership, I was simply eager to make a greater impact on K-12 education. I had the desire to work closely with teachers in the area of professional development, mentor our student-body instead of just my class roster, and to develop community connections. I wanted to help elevate our school's perception. Well, in my experience, all of the above was true of my principal at the time and I wanted to be just like her! She was bold, intelligent, and polarizing when she entered the room. She commanded your attention without saying a word. Ultimately, she is the reason I stepped outside of the comfort of teaching and became a school leader. I went on to pursue an advanced degree in education leadership.

In the early years of my teaching career journey I learned what not to do. Yes, that's right, I learned what not to do! When I became an assistant principal, I walked into the door inspired! As I reflect I realize I was faced with a bevy of behaviors I immediately knew not to replicate. I was exposed to leaders with a title, leaders that never left their offices, and leaders that loved to be the center of attention. I often thought to myself, "What about the students? What about their potential to be better people one day? What about the potential our entire school had to be higher performing?" What I observed did not take me down the road of successful leadership, instead it jarred me into taking notes on what did not work and on researching successful leaders that were making a difference in schools with similar demographics, performance data, and challenges. Despite recognizing lackluster leadership in the past, I was lucky enough to work alongside other school leaders that poured into me, trained me, shared their effective practices, and empowered me to keep going!

After serving four to five years as an assistant principal, in different districts, I moved to the university level and quickly realized I was in the wrong place! I moved back to the K-12 sector and into a principalship on the elementary level. After a difficult first principalship, I was later piloted into positions to work with teachers and students in underperforming schools. Leading turnaround efforts in failing and struggling schools is hard. Leadership is hard. I never would have imagined being purposed in leadership to serve high poverty, low performing schools. Yet, I would not seek any other type of school to lead and support. There's something about the challenge, the need for transformational leadership, and the hope of building teacher leadership that drives me here! Consequently, I've been afforded the opportunity to work with students whose backgrounds are similar to mine giving me even more of a charge to fight for them daily.

I am not at all ashamed of my experiences. I've made mistakes and I've learned from them. The key is be honest with yourself and make the necessary changes within yourself in order to truly see the depths of your school vision. A critical step for improvement as a leader is to identify a mentor. Someone that will listen, guide, and identify weaknesses through safe and constructive improvement efforts. I currently have a mentor that was assigned to me and I believe we were destined to work together. He can relate to my experiences, my thoughts, and my need to improve the school I serve. He listens intently and he gives critical feedback. Let me tell you how I had to grow to be willing to listen to someone I didn't have a prior relationship with and how liberating it is when we finish our sessions. One thing I've learned is that we have to become comfortable with being uncomfortable if we want to make a change for the better. Effective leaders can and should learn from other leaders.

Now here I am serving in my third struggling school and I believe I am equipped to lead in such perilous situations. Afterall, it was so easy to walk into schools that have it all together. The schools with large budgets, community support, parent involvement, consistent high performance on high-stakes assessments, and of course with a retention of highly-qualified teachers. My experiences have not been pretty. In fact, some of my experiences have been stained with struggle, loss, and lack of support, until the metamorphosis began to change the minds of the unbelievers! Those unbelievers had to see the real me and understand that my background could help make real change in the schools I serve. As I look back over my leadership journey, there are three critical steps I encourage all leaders to consider as you seek to build your teachers capacity and leadership toward excellence: **Create a community of leaders within your team, Courageously act and step out on faith, and Claim victory and celebrate the small wins.**

Building Teacher Capacity and Leadership for School Improvement

Create a community of leaders within your team.

Evaluating all areas of your organization is a critical first step in developing strategic steps for improvement. A valuable lesson I learned from other administrators is to develop a School Improvement Team (SIT) to assist you with identifying the needs and resources required to implement change. This will not only help you with your efforts it will allow you to empower teachers as leaders within your school. They will get a full understanding of the vision as they help develop it through the analysis of critical data, identification of resources, and actions steps needed to move the organization forward. In my experiences our SIT consisted of counselors, content area teachers, exceptional education teachers, interventionists, and anyone else that plays a significant role in the improvement of student learning outcomes.

Developing a school improvement plan is more than creating a detailed chart with action steps. It is the behind the scenes work that will truly develop your next steps to transform your school. Assign your novice teacher mentors and create opportunities for them to not only observe veteran teachers, but to meet in a setting that allows them to vent, ask questions, and have honest conversations. The teacher mentors often begin to develop their leadership ability and seek further opportunities to grow. These are the teachers that will seek licensure and move into the assistant principal or lead teacher roles for the future.

Courageously act and step out on faith!

Empower others to step up to the plate. Effective and purposeful professional development will not only yield buy-in, it can manifest into deeper collaboration and productivity for your teams. Tap into your staff and have them model lessons for one another. We have buildings with master teachers and best practices being shared every single day! What better way to foster a community of collaboration and sharing than to learn from each other. Listen to your team and give them a voice in decision-making and review of the organization. Your willingness to hear them and make necessary adjustments will give you credibility needed to take your school improvement efforts to the next level.

As you focus on collaboration and improvement, you will be able to identify those standing on the sidelines. Deal with your doubters head on or those that oppose the changes will eat you alive! Stand firm on your plan of action, continue clear communication with your school improvement team, and step out on faith with innovative ideas that align with growth and improvement. Push through the obstacles sent to kill your spirit daily. Your teacher leaders will help cheer on the sidelines. They will speak on your behalf because they believe in the vision.

Claim victory and celebrate the small wins!

Small wins are still wins. One thing I've learned over the years as an educational leader is to celebrate the small successes. Create an environment where people are recognized and celebrated for their success. Areas to consider include school-wide goals and achievement, teacher development, and community partnerships. Look within your school improvement team. Open meetings with kudos and positivity. Give team members the space and time to express themselves and celebrate their grade levels and/or departments.

We all know positivity is contagious so model it every way that you can. You will begin to see teachers highlight their successes in lesson development, implementation of new strategies, growth on interim assessment data, as well as improvement in their classroom cultures. When the organization begins to celebrate small wins they will be empowered to reach the once difficult goals and the school community will easily identify the transformation in your building. Leading turnaround efforts in failing and struggling schools is hard. Leadership is hard. Yet, we do it anyway and make a profound difference in the lives of children!

About Kristina Pollard

Kristina Pollard began her career in education in 1998 as a biology teacher in the Dallas Public School District. She has 22 years of experience, having served as a teacher, technology facilitator, assistant principal and principal in the elementary, middle and high school arenas. She also served as the Director of the H.E.L.P. for the College of Education at Marshall University.

She received a Bachelor of Science in biology from Jackson State University, a master's degree in elementary education from William Carey University and a specialist's degree in administrative leadership from Walden University.

She has received numerous grants and endowments used to fund educational initiatives in the schools she has served, and has received many awards and honors for her dedication to education. Most recently, she was named Forrest County School District Administrator of the Year in 2019 and currently serves on the Mississippi Department of Education Principal Advisory Board.

Kristina is the co-host of the Class Dismissed Podcast which discusses educational news and inspirational education ideas.

Ms. Shawaan Robinson

"I believe that it is necessary to create an environment where individuals feel comfortable expressing themselves freely without fear of judgment."
~ Shawaan Robinson

CHAPTER 6:

Leading From My Core

By Ms. Shawaan Robinson

My journey into educational leadership continues, 26 years after I entered my first classroom as an elementary school teacher. Currently as the acting principal of Briggs Chaney Middle School I possess a deep desire for the principalship in that I have the capacity to create systems designed for students to thrive and systems for staff to grow professionally. The unique skill set that I have acquired during my 26-year tenure as an educator from being a teacher, counselor, pupil personnel worker, assistant principal, principal intern allows me to successfully collaborate with school teams to reduce barriers to student learning and increase student access, opportunity, and achievement. Richard Dufour and Robert Marzano's words in (2011) Leaders of Learning, speak to my philosophy of leadership in that, "the best educational leaders are in love – in love with the work they do, with the purpose their work serves, and with the people they lead and serve" . As a school leader, I am deeply rooted in my core values and beliefs in *equity, shared leadership, culturally relevant pedagogy, student-centered learning, and relationship building.*

Equity

In an effort to be an impactful leader, I know that I must establish relationships with stakeholders that will inspire them to actualize and operationalize for equity. My goal to effectively examine and address personal belief systems remains at the forefront of my work. Building the capacity of teachers and staff to provide the best possible learning conditions for students to achieve especially students with learning differences and those that have been marginalized because of race and socioeconomic status is my primary focus. I operate on the premise that if my school were an educational utopia for Black, Hispanic, English Speakers of Other Languages (ESOL) and differently abled students, it would be a place where *cultural proficiency* is a mindset. The staff would embrace *cultural proficiency* as a paradigm shift from viewing cultural and learning differences as problematic to learning. I am inspired by the work of Glenn Singleton and Curtis Linton (2006) who suggest that "school leaders can become truly passionate for equity work as they discover a will to succeed with students of color in their school. Leaders with such passion will begin to see equity as an essential characteristic of their school's success ". I firmly believe that I have the capacity to effect change while knowing that I must balance my ideal state with the realities of the conditions that exist in school systems for minority students to fail. For this reason, I will continue to address patterns of inequity and act with purpose.

Culturally Relevant Pedagogy and Student-Centered Learning

While most school systems have moved away from a monocultural educational approach there is still a great need for the development of educators (teachers and leaders) with culturally relevant pedagogy. My work as a school leader is to support teachers in creating classrooms that value the experiences of students. I believe in student-centered learning which focuses on each student's needs, abilities, interests, and learning styles. Being truly passionate about facilitating and nurturing the conditions for teachers to close the opportunity gap for African American, Hispanic, ESOL and differently abled students, I aim to ensure that all students, particularly African American and Hispanic students thrive in a bias free learning environment and access culturally relevant curriculum, programs, materials and resources. I have a strong desire for my work to impact the development of the intellectual, interpersonal, emotional and social skills that my students will need to live, learn and work in a rapidly globalizing world. Additionally, it is equally important to me that the impact of my work in leading for equity and closing the opportunity and achievement gap for students will be sustainable. I consistently demonstrate my commitment to equity and student achievement by developing and implementing lasting instructional practices and programs.

Through deep discussions with staff, I continue to structure professional development to include tangible strategies on how to engage students in inquiry about subjects that matter to them as key features to employ to enhance the curriculum for their students. It is through these enhancements, that students will be able to access and relate to culturally relevant course content. I believe that opportunities to embed culturally relevant student-centered learning approaches into everyday teaching practices strengthens student motivation, promotes peer communication, reduces disruptive behavior, builds student-teacher relationships, and encourages active learning.

As an adjunct professor for McDaniel college, I am committed to supporting teachers and leaders in developing their culturally relevant pedagogy. Through teaching *Culturally Relevant Instruction and Leading for Equity and Excellence*, teachers and leaders are able to articulate what it means to be a culturally reflective practitioner and evaluate curriculum, pedagogy, assessment and learning environments in light of present practices in their schools and school systems. I guide them in developing culturally relevant practices to ensure access and opportunity for all students. I support teachers by identifying factors that contribute to writing a culturally relevant curriculum that incorporates diverse perspectives. Most importantly through this experience, I encourage and inspire teachers and leaders to act with intent to transform their practice to be more culturally reflective by cultivating a greater self-awareness of how racial and cultural identity impact performance which ultimately creates culturally relevant learning environments.

Shared Leadership

In my collaboration with stakeholders, I utilize facilitative leadership strategies to inspire commitment and lead highly effective teams. In order to achieve school success, shared governance of a school is necessary. Additionally, a school also needs more than one effective leader to be successful. The administrative team must responsible for taking a lead role in fostering a shared sense of ownership by articulating a clear vision and mission for the school, developing structures and consistently implementing processes. Knowing that everything I do each day can have a positive or negative influence on the students I serve, it is important that to value the student voice as being central and integral to the learning experience. I am certain that the success of shared leadership depends on the ability to build and manage productive collaborations with staff, students, parents and community partners.

Relationship Building

Dr. James Comer (1995) stated "no significant learning occurs without a significant relationship" . A school's culture thrives when there is a sense of community. Valuing a place where staff, students and parents feel as though their needs are being addressed timely and equitably, is crucial to the development of a trust-based climate and critical to staff morale and productivity. I believe that it is necessary to create an environment where individuals feel comfortable expressing themselves freely without fear of judgment. I value collaboration among professionals, positive interactions between staff and students and a mutual trust among parents and staff as being instrumental to student-centered education. In essence, student learning is the collective responsibility of the home, school, and community.

Moreover, my personal beliefs and core values manifest in my work as a visionary "warm demander" (Hammond, 2015) with the responsibility of ensuring that *all* students are held to high academic expectations and are valued and treated with respect. When working with teachers and staff, I communicate clear expectations regarding my instructional vision in that learning is truly a lifelong process and through effective professional learning communities (PLC) focused on equity, student success is inevitable. Finally, by establishing a rapport with families, I am able to gain their trust and assure them that I am truly committed to partnering with them in their child's education.

Analyzing Data Through the Lens of Equity: Best Practices Utilizing Stakeholder Feedback to Drive Instructional Practices

Utilizing stakeholder feedback to analyze data through the lens of equity is about relationships. As a leader, a key question to ask yourself as you analyze data is – *What relationships are affected by the outcomes of my decisions?* Establishing relational capital is what Shane Safir (The Listening Leader, 2017) describes as "a big savings account of trust and goodwill…to grow the account we must listen to people". Focusing on being a Listening Leader has allowed me to become more intentional and purpose driven in my leadership. This is a process I began to strengthen as an assistant principal through my utilization of *Blind Data Analysis*.

The process of blinding data is to conceal demographic information in an effort to analyze data objectively. Moreover, the aim of blinding is to eliminate or at best reduce bias. This process can be used to analyze both quantitative and anecdotal data. Thinking about the big picture, the outcomes that would serve all stakeholders, deepening listening skills promotes the development of a normed process for using data that will promote change, encourage questioning, improve practice, change structures, set policy, and ultimately provide access and opportunity for all students to thrive. Improving my ability to listen intently has allowed me to refine my analytical acumen, purposefully plan professional development that enhances data conversations, includes an examination of stakeholder beliefs, and supports planning for powerful instruction. As a result, I am able to operationalize and lead for equity with relationships at the core.

About Shawaan Robinson

Ms. Shawaan Robinson is the Acting Principal of Briggs Chaney Middle School in Silver Spring, MD. As the proud acting principal of Briggs Chaney-- home of the Bears, her vision simply states- **B**elieve in **E**quity, **A**ccess, and **R**igor for all **S**tudents! She is passionate about building relationships and creating the learning conditions for students to thrive.

Ms. Robinson has been an educator for 26 years and has worn many hats during her educational career. She has served as an elementary school teacher, elementary and middle school counselor, pupil personnel worker, assistant principal and principal intern working in diverse school communities. She is a doctoral student at the University of Maryland Eastern Shore. Her research is centered on the pathway to the secondary principalship for Black female administrators. She is passionate about establishing networks of support and expanding opportunities for Black women in educational leadership. She is an adjunct professor at McDaniel College in Western Maryland where she teaches *Leadership for Equity and Excellence.*

Ms. Robinson is a native of Washington, D.C. where she currently resides with her mom, two sons and an adorable pup.

LEADING FROM MY CORE

Mrs. Jewel Sanders

"A school culture should represent and promote positive relationships, effective teaching and learning, and college and career readiness."
-Mrs. Jewel Sanders

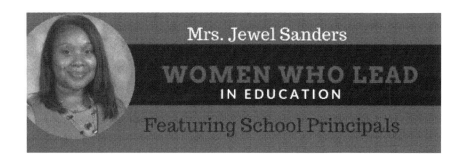

CHAPTER 7:

The Principalship

By Mrs. Jewel Sanders

On June 15, 2015, Jewel Sanders, was appointed the principal of Rosa M. Parks Middle School in Montgomery County Public Schools. That was a little over five years ago, and I'm still in shock. The previous year I served as the principal intern at the aforementioned school. The principal at the time was moving to a high school principalship which afforded me the opportunity to apply, interview, and ultimately become the principal. Transitioning into the new role stretched my leadership capacity with unexpected challenges that made me understand my influence with climate, community involvement, instruction, and professional development. The time arrived for me to define my *Leadership Philosophy*.

The second purpose of education...is to build bridges across the great divides, the so-called achievement gap, the technology gap, class divisions, the racial divide. If we do not find a way to bridge the divide between the haves and the have-nots, between white and black, between native and immigrant, then we are ensuring our ultimate demise. We are all part of the whole, and no part can be affected without affecting the whole (Delpit, 2012, p. 202).

As a leader who esteems specific principles and values in pedagogy, my philosophy aligns with Lisa Delpit. Unfortunately, I've seen students become disengaged in education because a bridge was never built, and they never felt valued nor found a connection to the educational environment. This feeling of disconnection and having a sense of being undervalued removes the student from the educational program emotionally and sometimes, physically. "Young people feel that who they are and what they want to become doesn't matter to teachers and schools. While students are required to fit into a restrictive school structure, culture, and curriculum, schools do little to fit themselves to their students" (Washor and Mojkowski, 2014). Being a principal at a universal design for learning (UDL) school, I learned to lead my staff, students, and community in promoting the necessity to support student learning and achievement by adhering to the three [UDL] guiding principles: give students various ways of acquiring information and knowledge; provide students alternatives for demonstrating what they know; and tapping into students' interests, offering appropriate challenges, and increasing motivation. As the visionary of the school, these principles can be followed as long as I continue to coordinate the efforts and the construction to build a bridge of opportunity for each and every student by creating a culture of integrity, engagement, collaboration and relationship building.

Integrity: Integrity is the thread that stitches my life experiences together. As a child I learned to tell the truth and to treat others the way I wanted to be treated. As an adolescent I learned that following the crowd was not always rewarded with positive popularity. As an adult I learned the importance of maintaining respectability and decorum. Integrity builds character and purpose. My belief in building a strong character, being honest and standing for what is right shapes who I am as a principal. The Greek philosopher, Heraclitus stated, "…The content of your character is your choice. Day by day, what you do is who you become. Your integrity is your destiny - it is the light that guides your way." By holding onto what is right, even when it's difficult, I am a principal who leads by example and creates a culture and the condition for each student to feel welcomed, valued and engaged.

Engagement: I focus on being the principal of a school where students are engaged and where connections are made among students, teachers and course studies. But the engagement is not defined solely by receiving passing grades, but by each student's interest in the school community. I expect each student to become involved with the extra-curricular programs in addition to the academics. I expect each student to identify a special quality or personality trait in each of his/her teachers that informs him/her that the teacher cares. Students have opportunities to be leaders within the school setting, while extending that leadership into the community and beyond. Each student knows he/she matters. As a result of this expectation, my school provides myriad school programs to which students can become active.

Collaboration: It is my job, along with my leadership team, to create and model an environment where it is common practice for teachers to collaborate and to optimally function in professional learning communities, to "deliver content and skills in a rich way that genuinely improve outcomes for students" (Rotherham & Daniel, 2009). Teachers engage each other in pedagogical dialogue, share ideas, analyze student data and conduct peer observations to ensure that each student is learning. Students engage in student-centered discourse which promotes collaborative thinking and leadership / ownership of their learning. I work with my staff to plan community events which conveys a message that the school walls extend into the community. Student growth and development become the priority of all stakeholders: parents, staff, students and the community.

Relationships: As a staff, we must build personal relationships with students. Teachers must set high expectations for student learning and for how they [teachers] address students' needs. In a world where differences in cultures, socio-economic status, abilities, etc. exist, instructional practices should address the variances in students' abilities and students' prior knowledge.

As the principal, I must create and maintain "a welcoming, intellectually stimulating environment in which all students will demonstrate significant growth in their abilities to think critically, act responsibly, and contribute positively within diverse settings" (montgomeryschoolsmd.org/schools/rosaparksms/principal/). To accomplish this task, the entire school community has to buy into the vision. Part of my role as principal, depends on me fostering a climate where students, staff, parents, and the community feel valued, as well as understand their part of making and keeping the vision alive. To do this, I provide transparent leadership. When possible, I consistently include all stakeholders in decision making matters by way of surveys, town-halls, meetings, and informal discussions. I participate in community events to convey the school community extends beyond the school building. Additionally, I communicate regularly with the school community.

As an instructional leader, I lead the school discussions and creation of a master schedule that allows for departments and teams to engage in collaborative planning for students to access high-quality instruction. The schedule allows for students with disabilities and English Language Learners (ELLs) to have supported classes. The schedule provides opportunities for extended learning and interventions. I have coached department resource teachers in their positions as teacher leaders to implement culturally proficient instruction and to maintain a high functioning instructional program. I conduct informal and formal observations to determine areas for growth in the instructional program and support underperforming teachers by implementing professional growth plans.

I co-lead professional development sessions for staff to inform their job performance. Professional development is provided for all staff: teachers, para-educators, secretaries, and building service workers. All staff engage in race and equity training to challenge belief systems, impact student achievement, and promote diversity. I coordinate parent workshops to positively support the influence parents have on their children.

A school culture should represent and promote positive relationships, effective teaching and learning, and college and career readiness. Students will be ready to progress beyond high school if the bridge of integrity, engagement, collaboration and relationship building is built. As a school leader, I stand at the core of this vision, helping staff, students, parents, and the community access the bridges that promote excellence and equity for each student.

About Mrs. Jewel Sanders

Mrs. Jewel Sanders is an equity warrior who has had 25 years of experience in education. She's a native New Yorker and has worked in three different school systems as a teacher, parent/community liaison, department chair, staff development teacher, administrator, and currently, a middle school principal at Rosa Parks Middle School in Montgomery County Public Schools. Mrs. Sanders believes in inspiring and nurturing student leaders. She sponsors a Student Diversity Leadership Team (SDLT). This group of students works in and outside the school to focus on providing equity and a welcoming environment for all students. She's created a platform for SDLT to partner with other student leadership groups and / or outside organizations to lead a diversity conference for middle school students, facilitate school-wide lessons centering around films on diversity and /or character building, survey peers to capture student voice data, and so much more! She wrote the article, *Student Leadership: A Principal's Point of View* in 2019, a response to the school shooting in Parkland, Florida.

Mrs. Sanders earned a Bachelor of Arts in English and minored in Africana Studies at the State University of New York at Albany (SUNY Albany), and a Master's Degree in English Education at Teachers College, Columbia University. She currently is a doctoral candidate at University of Maryland, Eastern Shore.

Mrs. Tammy Taylor

"...I have found it to be true that my school culture is always at work. The culture is always at work, either helping or hindering learning."
~Tammy Taylor

CHAPTER 8:

Built To Last: Creating A Culture And Climate Of Excellence

By Mrs. Tammy Taylor

As a school leader, I believe two of the most essential aspects of a successful school are healthy school culture and positive school climate. Some scholars may debate whether these two notions should be considered one and the same; however, I subscribe to a different school of thought, as my experiences have taught me these two concepts are independent variables of a school's identity. Although the two are not the same, research supports culture and climate are interrelated phenomena having a reciprocal impact on each other; yet they are very different ideologies. As such, it can be said, culture and climate are two very different aspects of a school's persona. The Alliance for Education Solutions defines school culture as the ways things are done in the school (the personality of a school), the underlying norms and values that shape patterns of behavior, attitudes, and expectations between stakeholders in the school. They go on to say, Deal and Peterson (1998) say school culture includes "norms, values, beliefs, traditions, and rituals built up over time." Many educational organizations have produced detailed descriptions of positive school cultures, as well as strategies for improving them. As an administrator, I have learned the most important aspect of developing a healthy culture is knowing exactly who and what creates that culture. I have discovered getting to know the staff, students, parents, and the community you serve is a great place to start. After taking the time to get to know your school family, as an administrator, you can begin to prioritize, create protocols, adopt practices, and set expectations that support your belief in the ability of every student. In creating these school-wide expectations and norms, your school's culture will begin to take shape.

On the other hand, school climate can be defined as the feel of the school (the school's attitude), the behaviors and points of view exhibited and experienced by students, teachers, and other stakeholders. Freiberg and Stein (1999) describe school climate as "the heart and soul of the school," the feeling that either encourages teachers and students to engage, love the school, and want to be a part of it, or to reject the school and disengage from it. School climate is actually the outcome of the school's norms and values, the way in which the people at the school relate to and interact with one another, and the way systems and policies manifest themselves. The climate in my building has gone from being one of toxicity, frustration, and anxiety, to being one of positive optimism, support, collaboration, and peace. As a conscientious school leader, I have found it to be true that my school culture is always at work. The culture is always at work, either helping or hindering learning. It influences every decision and action in my school, from the way I lead to the way the teachers use their time to plan, deliver instruction, monitor progress, and interact with one another, as well as students and their parents.

Every administrator wants to have the legacy of having led a successful school. Therefore, much of their time and energy (and many times their resources) are poured into the instructional program at the school. Instruction is very important and certainly does matter a great deal when identifying successful schools. However, if the culture of the building is unhealthy, it is nearly impossible to see a school excelling in any area, because most of the time, the teachers are not fully committed.

As educators, we are all familiar with the work of John Hattie, and as such we know that the single factor that has the greatest impact on students' academic success is teacher efficacy. Knowing this fact, I spent the entire first year as a principal trying to create a culture of excellence in my school. I spent time getting to know my staff, my students and their parents, and acclimating myself to a new community. I realized very quickly, in order to develop a healthy and productive culture, I was going to have to be methodical in my approaches and move slowly to get the levels of commitment that would be necessary for us to create an excellent school while getting people in the right places.

As simple as that may sound, the process was actually very complicated and required me to have to do some soul searching and introspection about my own personal biases, inhibitions, trepidations, and preconceived notions. I knew that in order for us to move the school forward, it would require two very important things. The first and a very important thing we would have to do was establish trust. I knew the staff would have to learn to trust me and my leadership, while I learned to trust them. This had to include their judgment, instructional practices, intentions, actions, and their hearts. The second, equally important, thing we would have to do was exorcise all of the toxins from the current culture. Toxins are everywhere, and yes, they come to school with people. Therefore, we had to be willing to address all of the impediments impeding our beliefs that our students were able to learn and perform at high levels. What types of toxins had to be exorcised is a question you may be asking yourself at this point. I have an answer. Those toxins included racism, classism, misunderstandings, closed mindedness, competition, distrust, passive aggressiveness, fixed mindsets, and the list could go on and on. What I just described probably sounds like a horrible place to have to go and work, surprisingly and quite to the contrary, it was not. The staff was a great staff, composed of some amazing people. The reality is those toxins exist in every organization, and only a few people with a transformational mindset are willing to challenge them by facing them head on. Fortunately for me, I am one of those transformational people. I knew that a healthy culture was not going to simply happen, but I was going to have to intentionally create the space for that culture to be cultivated. Our journey towards real trust in a student-centered environment was not an easy one. It was my responsibility to create an environment built on synergy by coaching my folks to change through the strengths of my leadership. Some staff members were immediately on board, while others were not. Many people decided they didn't want to work towards the goals that had been set forth, and those folks decided to move on. I respected and supported those decisions. As an administrator, at this crucial time, I was forced to face some harsh realities about myself before I could truly become an agent of change. I am a chaos free individual. I have always tried my best to avoid conflict, not because I am afraid of it, but because it disturbs my energy. Simply put, I don't like it. However, during my self-reflection and hopes of discovering the best way to effect a needed change at my school I realized that in order to develop real trust, you actually have to have conflict or an unhealthy false sense of harmony is created. In this type of environment there is absolutely no conflict and everyone goes about their business as though life is great. However, deep down everybody secretly despises at least one thing about everybody else. I had to lead my staff on a path to being able to engage in constructive conflict. In order for us to not create an environment of destructive conflict, we spent time really looking at the conflict continuum and establishing norms so that we knew how to settle matters before there was any destruction. I welcomed staff members to share their thoughts and opinions with me especially when they differed from mine. We learned how to agree that we don't agree and not have any hard feelings as a result, and they learned not to fear me revengefully retaliating against them for voicing their opinions or disagreeing with something I had suggested. They also learned that differing opinions didn't make us enemies, but could help us to learn tolerance, respect, and provide an opportunity to gain perspective. We committed to subscribing to a philosophy of accountability (with ALL of us being accountable for student achievement) and moved away from finger-pointing and blaming each other. We adopted a philosophy of respect and support, and developed a growth mindset for all.

A harder and more difficult aspect of culture to navigate during that time was changing the way the staff viewed competing. I am an avid sports fan, so I respect and appreciate the spirit of competition. Growing up in a household with three brothers who had strong convictions about three different NFL teams, I learned the definition of competition very early. However, in a school setting, there really is no place for competition in the sports' sense of competing. In education there should be camaraderie and collaboration to help us all to continually learn, grow, and improve. I had the task of helping my staff to realize, we are only as successful as our lowest performing class. I spent countless hours in professional development with my staff ensuring they understood in order for there to be collective teacher efficacy in our school, we would have to learn to work together. It took a little time to get the primary teachers to understand we were all accountable for our state test data and learn to accept their role in the academic challenges we were facing as a school. We stopped looking at things from a single class perspective and began to view our data as grade level teams. This has created a sense of collaboration and now our teams complete a weekly collaboration log to assist them in their plans to meet the needs of all of our students, and it allows me to have an active role in the collaboration. Although the staff is largely comprised of new staff members, the level of commitment and intentionality is incredible. There is no better staff to be found, of course, I am quite biased. I can honestly say a turning point for me as a principal that led me to a point of self-assessing and began my transformation as a leader occurred after a conversation with Principal Baruti Kafele at a small group meeting he conducted in Charlotte, North Carolina. During the discussion, he looked directly at me and asked, "Young lady, is your school a better school because you lead it?" I am aware he wasn't talking specifically to me, but rather to all of the amazing leaders in that room (who all happened to be females); however, I took the question to heart. For weeks I asked myself that question, and I always came to the same conclusion: "I think it is." That strengthened my resolve and emboldened me to make sure that everyone else would not just think it – but would know it, as well. I started leading like an influencer, because I knew I was there to make things better. That became my mission. I wanted every aspect of my school to improve, and it did. From that time until this moment, I proudly say without hesitation, my school is absolutely better because I lead it.

Creating a culture of excellence is not an easy task for sure; however, I am proof that it can be done. After creating a culture of collaboration and high expectations in my school, our school ended up with scores in the bottom 5 percent of the state that year, throwing us into School Improvement as a result of an Unsatisfactory rating on our state report card. This was a demoralizing blow to the school, for sure, but to me, the blow was almost debilitating. I don't lose. I wasn't designed to fail. I am a winner, because winning is what I do. These are not just positive affirmations, but simply the way things are. I had the privilege of growing up and marrying into a family where winning was encouraged and expected. My mother, my grandmother, my grandfather, my brothers, my aunts, my uncles, my cousins, my neighbors. and my church family have provided a safety net for me to always work towards being my best self. I come from a long line of strong and courageous women. My mom, my biggest champion, taught me to never settle. I have always been encouraged to aim high, knowing anything is possible because I believe. As such, failure has not and will never be an option for me. However, I need to be transparently honest. For a brief moment, I was shaken, I actually wasn't sure exactly what I was going to do. I questioned my decision to work on making cultural shifts to lead us to academic achievement. I felt like giving up, but I knew my mission, and as such, I was committed to staying the course and ensuring my staff did not allow our newly assigned label to set us back. I thought back on a sermon my husband once preached and encouraged myself, "I might bend, but I can't break, because I was built to last!" At that point, I knew exactly what I had to do. I immediately rolled up my sleeves.

Being named a Comprehensive Support and Improvement (CSI) School was like being branded with my own Scarlet A. Although I was willing to wear that Scarlet letter, I refused to allow it to be assigned to my staff or students. Every opportunity I got, I celebrated them and bragged about how awesome they were. We took a lashing on Social Media outlets and in the conversations of other administrators and staff throughout my district; however, I refused to succumb to speculations and rumors, because I knew what was happening in my school. Consequently, I was keenly aware of how easily this single episode could have completely destroyed the culture of excellence I was working so hard to create. I decided that I had to maintain my focus on creating a culture of excellence, and I could only do so by encouraging my staff to recognize that every school needs to improve and our competition was only going to be against ourselves so that we would always be in a position to get better. We simply didn't have time to waste worrying about what was happening in other schools or what other people were saying about us. Although, that was my message to the staff, in reality, that was not how we were being compared or viewed. I refused to allow my staff and students to be exposed to what I decided was buffoonery. Being a school in improvement is not a fun place to be; however, two very beneficial things resulted from our being named a CSI school. The first is we received a large sum of money, as a result. Receiving these funds allowed us to do some things that we would not have been able to do without them. Secondly, our designation came with a state transformation coach being assigned to our school. Of course, this was another reason for much of the chatter circulating about the district, more than likely because no one knew what being assigned a transformation coach actually meant. Personally, I embraced the idea. I am (and was) of the mindset, I will do whatever it takes to improve my school. Upon meeting my coach, I knew there had been divine intervention, as we immediately connected. She's a retired principal from another state with a wealth of knowledge in almost every aspect of leadership. I have learned so many things from her that have solidified my practices as a leader. She has been a tremendous resource to me personally, but also to my school. She could see I was doing everything I could to support my staff and keep them encouraged and motivated to keep pushing. She could also see I was doing everything I was doing on my own, while my success was being judged only in comparison to other schools. She encouraged me to focus on only the things I had control over and to pour my energy and efforts into those things.

After thinking about my coach's advice, I knew a flawed accountability system that compared me to someone else was not going to do anything to help me improve. I realized I would have to find a support system (a part from her) on my own. A space where true collaboration and support could take place free of competition and discouragement. That support came through a like-minded colleague, I call her my "trust-mate", who believed what I believed about the power of collaboration and supporting each other. That collaboration has led us to hosting weekly The Collaborative, an online platform to provide a collaborative space for parents, teachers, and school leaders to gain perspective from one another and work together to solve some of the issues we are currently facing in education. Someone may be asking why this is important. I can tell you why from my perspective. Collaborating with my "trust-mate", standing firm on my faith, drawing strength from my family, taking advantage of the wisdom and expertise of my coach, keeping my staff and students encouraged, maintaining high expectations for all, having an Instructional Team that was as committed to me as they were to my vision and who learned to trust me as their leader, while believing in myself and knowing I was doing what I had been assigned to do furthered us on our journey to excellence. Our school went from being an Unsatisfactory School in the bottom 5 percent of the state to being rated a Good (almost Excellent) School in just a single year. As a person of faith, I know from whence my help comes. As a family-oriented individual, I also know that without the love, support, encouragement, and solidarity provided by my family, I would have crumbled beneath all of the pressure. However, instead of abandoning my assignment; I was able to look to the hills for the help I needed to change the trajectory of my school. It also helped that during this time, I was blessed with the constant company of two very needed distractions, Little Miss Abigail and Little Miss Addison with Dorien playing in the background. I am very fortunate, during this time, I was also able to discover the true power of genuine collaboration.

In our book (my "trust-mate" and I are co-authors), It Doesn't Have to Be Lonely at the Top: The Power of Collaboration, we share some of the experiences that led us to pen the details of our journeys in hopes we will be able to help someone else to find a "trust mate" and recognize the power of collaborating. Collaboration and support will profit and benefit individuals, for sure. Honestly, collaboration and support are two tools that can change schools and the world of education as we now know it. In the book, I describe in more detail why I had to work double time to ensure my staff didn't lose their faith in themselves or the processes we had put into place when a devastating event occurred that could have destroyed our school culture as we knew it. In the book, I also share how during one of the saddest events in my life, I had to choose whether I could allow myself time to wallow and retreat, the way I felt like doing, or if I was going to save my school. As you might guess, I chose the latter. Grab a copy of the book – It Doesn't Have to Be Lonely at the Top: The Power of Collaboration - to read that story and many others that speak to the power of a healthy school culture and positive school climate, as well as having a strong support system and true and genuine collaboration. Throughout my life, I have learned, even when things don't go exactly the way we would like them to or there is an unexpected detour on our paths to destiny, we should always stay true to who we are. I would encourage you to grant yourself permission to be who you have been created to be without fear or trepidation, and I hope like me, you may find peace in knowing, all of God's promises are Yes and Amen to the Glory of God - 2 Corinthians 1:20.

About Tammy Taylor

Tammy Taylor is a dedicated educator who has committed her life and career to the service of others. She is an elementary principal in South Carolina.

Tammy is currently pursuing her Ph.D. from the University of South Carolina. Her passion for validating the experience of the principalship and the impact on students' achievement, drives her research focus. This research will focus on the leadership experiences of four African American, female principals and their experiences: challenges and successes.

Tammy is married to Pastor Keith Taylor. She has worked faithfully to support him in ministry for over two decades. She's passionate about working with youth, and has worked with young ladies to create a sense of value and self-worth through teaching them to understand, accept, and fulfill their purposes in life. She has become known for her work with a youth organization - at their church, Girls All About Purpose (GAAP).

Dr. L. Jackie Tobias

"Great administrators are like great chefs. They spend an inordinate amount of time preparing, planning, and visioning before they begin to cook or implement." - Dr. Jackie Tobias

CHAPTER 9:

The Secret Ingredient to

A Successful School - A Great Culture

By Dr. L. Jackie Tobias

I have been an educator for over 30 years; I am beginning my 11th year as a principal. I spent my early years as a counselor starting in elementary school, moving to middle and then to high school. I was not the person that you would expect to be an educator. In fact, I hated high school. My family migrated to America when I was 17 and I entered high school in America for the second half of my senior year. Suffice it to say it was not a pleasant experience and I endured not only culture shock but also loneliness of alienation as a 17-year-old. Basic American culture, I did not understand and particularly the nuances of high school were foreign to me. A prom, SAT, lunch and classroom protocols, were things I had to learn, not to mention the fact that I belonged to had no social group. I barely survived, those six months. I got into college because of my high school counselor, saw something in me, the ability to succeed, and assisted me in applying to University of Florida. This was the beginning of my "calling" as an educator. This is a ministry for me. I take pride in enabling children to succeed as someone did for me. I went on to graduate with a masters and specialist in counseling. I followed later with a master's degree in administration and culminating in my doctorate degree in educational leadership. I am particularly proud of the fact that I persisted and got a doctorate. I was the student who no one thought would succeed, who was overlooked in class and thus became unmotivated. I represent all the children who believe they cannot, because no one believes in them. I started this by saying my profession is a calling, I am called to provide structures for students to become their best.

As I read my own story, I drive myself to become an expert in helping children succeed to put structures in place so teachers are equipped to assist students like myself, whom no one thought would succeed. I have become an expert in moving schools that are low performing and enhancing schools with middle to low performing students. I have also become an expert in motivating teachers to be successful for students. I can efficiently build collaborative learning environments where teachers feel empowered and supported. The key to student achievement is having the right people at the table, growing, and supporting them in a positive culture with high expectations.

I have been at my current school for six years. When I started there, we were performing well based on North Carolina standards, but the climate was very "cold". The teachers and students were doing what they had to do. There was not a sense of doing the work because we "loved" our school and community. Currently the culture has changed to one in which teachers are empowered and are encouraged to be collaborative leaders. The teacher turnover rate is consistently less than 2 percent. The positive climate is palpable when you walk into the building. Students know that they can be a part of changes in the schools they are expected to perform at a high standard and they own their academic success. We have now improved to being an A+ school for the last six years, and making double digit growth every year, based on State standards. We have been second and fifth in the State in student growth. I am most proud that I have been the facilitator of our A status and upward growth. It is not easy to be proficient and to grow our students. I do want to add that based on the State report card only 34% of our 9th grade students come prepared for high school. Currently 100 percent of our seniors graduate and the majority choose to attend two or four-year College. Growing our students, while achieving our A status is one of my proudest achievements. I am more proud of the collaborative, empowered positive culture of high expectations that I have had the pleasure to serve.

"Great administrators are like great chefs. They spend an inordinate amount of time preparing, planning, and visioning before they begin to cook or implement. During this time, they keep their focus on the outcomes and the clients. They continuously re-adjust, refocus and re-evaluate their plans and efforts." – N.A. Connors. Captured in that quote is my vision for leading a successful school. Keeping staff focused on the "real work" takes deliberate and thoughtful preparation. Creating a culture of high expectations is the beginning of keeping staff focused on learning, instruction, and assessment.

"Building a school culture of trust is an intentional act that benefits principals, teachers, and students." – Jane Moodono. As I reflect on how my leadership fosters an atmosphere of trust and mutual respect, the word intentional screams at me from this quote. Building trust and mutual respect must be intentional and an integral part of great leadership. The quote resonates with me, as I believe that developing trust and mutual respect is foundational to building healthy relationships that then ultimately leads to student success.

I am very conscious that successful schools are because you have the "right people on the team." This is not as simple as it sounds because you have to grow, support and challenge those on the team to ensure the success of our students. Creating an open and collaborative environment begins with my behavior and disposition. I have to model respect for my colleagues, I value their professional judgement and I encourage them to communicate openly with administration and one another. Teachers are expected to act as the professionals that they are and I believe people live up to your expectations of them. I strive to create an environment where they know that I value what they do. I am there to serve them and I communicate that openly. I ensure that all staff have materials necessary for them to complete their work and I go over and above to create an atmosphere where we are family and treat each other respectfully. For example, I started the Teacher of the Month, where the teachers choose a peer, someone who they do not usually work with; they pass them a glass apple as respect for their work. This is a small example of a simple activity to allow peers to acknowledge each other and to promote a spirit of collegiality. The staff is not micromanaged but encouraged to develop their areas of strength, to be innovative and creative and to feel empowered to contribute to the greater good of the school.

I also use surveys given by our State, such as the North Carolina Teacher Working Conditions Survey or our student climate surveys, which gauge trust and respect. I am open and honest by putting the data out front and asking for suggestions, to ensure that we address any weakness in those areas. This has to be a joint and transparent school activity. Teacher's need to have the ability to analyze the school, themselves and myself and to provide meaningful suggestions for improvement.

Every year my staff is "whisked" away to a location away from the building for a "staff retreat." The location is chosen specifically so staff will feel like they are professionals on a learning retreat. We have gone to the beach, to a four-star golf resort and to various high-end conference centers. The point is that they will feel and know that they are treated as professionals because I chose a venue that is "worthy" for their growth. Professional learning and development starts with how people are treated. A venue is a simple thing but it says a lot about the expectation and learning that I expect from the staff. The environment away from the building encourages staff to bond and honestly contemplate the vision, mission and focus of our school. Open communication is encouraged, and staff are empowered to have a voice. Creating a safe professional space is a part of my building trust and mutual respect, along with professional development activities that foster openness. Differentiated opportunities for growth and learning begins with who organizes the retreat. The retreat is the same, but different each year. The difference in the agenda is based on the staff. A younger staff, with less experience changes the offerings and the structure of the retreat. For example, I would focus on management, building relationships and developing school culture with new staff. With a veteran staff, the offerings are catered to deeper insights into critical thinking and brain research, which are examples of topics that have been discussed previously. Knowing your staff and staff needs professionally and developmentally is key to providing appropriate professional development. I also empower the leadership team to be an integral part of the decision-making and organization of the retreat. They are an interdisciplinary group of leaders in the school that have a pulse on the developmental and professional knowledge, skills and practices needed for the year. Please note that I choose people who also need this developmentally as they are leaders. Our leadership team reflects every year on what would benefit our school and students. Last school year, for example, our data showed that our Hispanic students were consistently struggling in reading comprehension. The team decided that the faculty needed professional development to ensure that everyone had strategies to target this particular weakness. The theme for this school year was "Personalized Education." We were striving to meet our personal academic and performance goals for students and staff alike. We brought in speakers to address the needs of all of our students who struggle with reading comprehension, not just those of Hispanic descent. The professional development was directed at all staff, as it was an area of need for everyone. We also have conference type sessions geared at specific needs and concerns. Staff members who have been successful in this area and who have volunteered to share their own best practices facilitate the other sessions. This year due to COID, clearly technology and meeting our students' needs is at the forefront of discussion. Our meetings focus on staff sharing strengths and open discussion on mitigating student academic and emotional losses. We are a professional learning community; all learning is based on the needs of the school, broken down by students or staff deficient. The success that we have exhibited at my school is due first to a culture of high expectations, where teachers are treated with care and value as professionals. The professional learning provided is scripted and it is because I am fully aware that the teachers are different and have different needs. As a leader, my goal is to capitalize on providing differentiated learning for all our growth.

I foster trust and mutual respect by getting to know the staff not only professionally but also personally. I meet with every teacher individually at the beginning of the year, to discover their professional goals but to encourage the pursuit of personal goals. I am very transparent and usually share my goals for the year first. My office is always open and I welcome thoughts, ideas and suggestions to make us better. I try to make it my business to try to "say yes," or how can I assist you with accomplishing it. Active listening to all stakeholders is an important skill and one that I practice often, care is often easily communicated by just listening. As a leader, I have to "give away" some power to ensure that conditions are created to empower my teachers; this goes a long way in creating a trusting and respectful environment.

Visibility is another key element in fostering trust and respect. I do not believe you can effectively lead a school from your office. I am in the hallways, classrooms and the cafeteria frequently. I get to know staff and students by interacting with them in the hallways, classrooms and the cafeteria. Authentic, trust, and respect will not exist if the school community does not see me listening, laughing, interacting, tweeting and caring about them. Frequent walkthroughs foster authentic discussions, even when they are crucial conversations, because visibility fosters trust and respect. Walkthroughs occur daily and practical feedback is given to teachers related to processes of learning and the instruction that occurs in the classroom. Teachers expect that after formal and informal observations, feedback to improve their instruction and student learning.

As with a good chef, I continually "prep" our staff to look at their students individually, to look at data, and to reassess strategies to meet the students' needs on an individual level. These processes are to make our teachers better perfect their craft so they can better serve our students and advocate for the authenticity of the students' experiences. I personally meet with every teacher to discuss professional and academic goals. I also discuss any needs that will assist them in ensuring that they can perform their jobs at an optimal level. I have frequent daily walkthroughs and teachers are given electronic feedback before I even leave the room. If there are issues of concern, I meet with teachers face-to-face. Our conversations are typically a candid discussion based on the premise that we are here to grow as professionals. Our ultimate goal is to ensure that all teachers are operating on a high level to provide lessons that spur critical thinking and challenge students intellectually. Keeping staff focused on learning, instruction and assessment begins with strategic course scheduling and student placement. This collaborative planning ensures that our schedule is effective and assists teachers with learning and planning. Scheduling starts before the school year ends as teacher teams must look at student data and provide suggestions for effective student scheduling. This keeps achievement at the forefront and is governed by the philosophy that teachers are an integral part of making their schedules, and ensures that students are given optimal opportunities for success. In addition, where common planning is possible I strive to ensure that we build a schedule that allows teachers the opportunity to collaborate and plan. Our schedule is planned using student data as a guide, we build in bridge courses and place students strategically in classes to enhance their success. As an instructional leader I have to always model what I expect from the staff. I inspire them by keeping instruction, learning and assessments at the forefront of our conversations. When I have discussions with teachers or teams, my questions always go back to those main themes. We always focus on students, which is the "real work." I believe that education has to be personal, has to be authentic, has to be relevant and has to challenge our students. I believe that it also has to be this way for the adults, who support the students.

Dysfunctions of a Team by Patrick Lencioni he outlines the elements needed to build strong, cohesive teams. Trust is the foundation; I certainly support and work hard to ensure that trust along with mutual respect are the foundations that I fostered every day, to build a great school culture and in turn a great school.

My motto is that it "takes a village to raise a child" and my goal is always to ensure that all the villagers are supported in their journey to raise productive, thoughtful, and capable children. The following quote summarizes my view on building successful schools and I challenge all educators to take this to heart.

"When we come to believe that our schools should be providing a school culture that creates and sustains a community of student and adult learning--that this is the trellis of our profession--then we will organize our schools, classrooms, and learning experiences differently. Show me a school where instructional leaders constantly examine the school's culture and work to transform it into one

hospitable to sustained human learning, and I'll show you students who do just fine on those standardized tests. "A school's culture has more influence on life and learning in the schoolhouse than the president of the country, the state department of education, the superintendent, the school board, or even the principal, teachers, and parents can ever have." - Roland Barth From Farrington, C.A., Roderick, M., Allensworth, E., et. al, Teaching Adolescents to Become Learners: The Role of Non-Cognitive Factors in Shaping School Performance

About Dr. L. Jackie Tobias

Dr. Jackie Tobias has been an educator for over 30 years and she is in her eleventh year as a principal. She spent her early years as a counselor starting in elementary school, moving to middle and then later, to high school. She was not the person that one would expect to be an educator. In fact, she hated high school.

Her family migrated to America when she was 17 and she entered high school in America for the second half of her senior year. She barely survived high school, but she managed to get into college because of her high school counselor, who saw something in her: the ability to succeed, and assisted her in applying to the University of Florida. This was the beginning of her "calling" as an educator. She considers this her ministry. She takes pride in enabling children to succeed as someone did for her.

She went on to graduate with Bachelor's, Master's and Specialist degrees in Education and School Counseling. She followed later with a Master's degree in School Administration from University of North Carolina in Greensboro. Her formal education culminated with a Doctoral degree in Educational Leadership from Gardner Webb University. She is driven to become an expert in helping children succeed and to put structures in place so teachers are equipped to assist students like herself, who no one thought would succeed.

Dr. Tobias is the 2020 Durham Public Schools Principal of the Year.

VISIONARY AUTHOR

Dr. Sharon H. Porter

ABOUT THE VISIONARY

Dr. Sharon H. Porter (Dr. Sharon) is the President of SHP Enterprise, the umbrella entity of Perfect Time SHP LLC, Coaching, Consulting, and Book Publishing Form and SHP Media and Broadcasting. She is the Executive Director and Founder of The Next In Line to Lead Aspiring Principal Leadership Academy (APLA), where she trains, mentors, and coaches assistant principals from across the United States who desire to take the helm as principal.

Dr. Sharon is Co-Founder, owner, and Editor-In-Chief of Vision & Purpose LifeStyle Magazine. She is the Vice-President of V&P Media and cohosts the V&P Inspiring Our Community Podcast. Dr. Sharon is the host of The I Am Dr. Sharon Show, Let's Talk Politics with Dr. Sharon, The Book Talk Show, It's All Business, and Education FIRST. She is a founding partner of the What Now Movement and serves as Chief Communication Officer and Vice-President of Media and Marketing for WNM Ventures, LLC.

She is a lifelong public educator, with over 25 years of experience as an elementary and middle school principal, Leadership Development Coach, assistant principal, Instructional Specialist, Curriculum Coordinator and elementary and middle school classroom teacher. Dr. Sharon is the author, visionary, and publisher of The Next in

Line to Lead book series, The Women Who Lead Book series, Young Ladies Who L.E.A.D. and The HBCU Experience Anthology, book series.

Dr. Sharon is a graduate of Howard University, Walden University, Johns Hopkins University, National-Louis University, and Winston-Salem State University. She is a part of the 2019 Harvard University School of Education Women in Leadership Cohort.

She is an official member of the Forbes Coaches Council, International Association of Women (IAW), American Business Women's Association, Professional Women of Winston-Salem, and Delta Sigma Theta Sorority, Inc.

You can connect with her on Facebook, Twitter, Instagram, and LinkedIn.

Made in the USA
Middletown, DE
24 February 2021